Sarah

Esther Vliegenthart

Written by:
Esther Vliegenthart

Illustrated by:
Esther Vliegenthart

Translated by:
Susanne Chumbley

Published by:
Graviant educational publications,
Doetinchem, The Netherlands

© August 2016

ISBN 978-9491337901

Introduction

I am a proud mother of two lovely daughters and a beautiful son. My son has Autism and sees the world differently than we do. He experiences sound, images and touch completely differently than I do. This was very noticeable when he was young. He sometimes wanted me to read a story to him, but would rather not look at the brightly coloured pictures or the images of the characters of the book that looked at him directly from it. Sometimes the stories could also upset him and cause more chaos in his mind than he already experienced. We didn't directly notice this, but now he is 7, we have learned a lot more about him and now know that a lot of the pre-school books were not suitable for him. I, as a literacy lover, find it a shame and would love to see that all children can enjoy stories and the illustrations.

That is why I wanted to create a book that makes children feel safe and makes them calm by recognising a story that doesn't ask for their own interpretation, so it will prevent that reading a book will raise more questions and insecurity than they already had. But above all, I wanted to create a book that will teach these children; you are beautiful and perfect, the way you are!

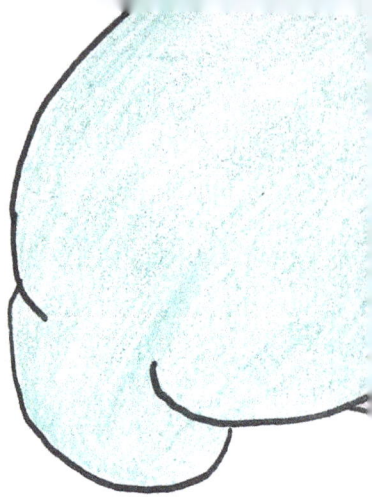

In the middle of the forest
Just past the toadstool scene
Is a sweet little squirrel house
You probably see what I mean

That is where Sarah and her parents live
With her little toy mouse
And when daddy goes out to work
Sarah stays with her mum at their house

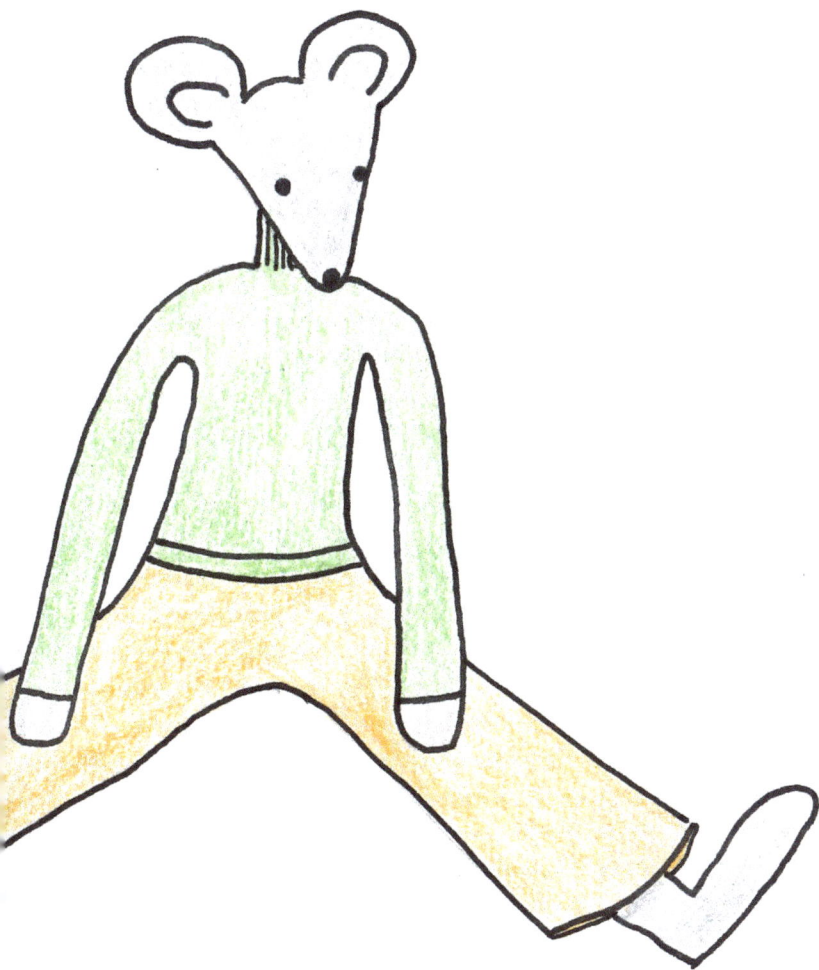

Mummy does the cleaning
And makes everything spick and span
Sarah has to play by herself
As good as she possibly can

Sarah finds it difficult
To choose what she likes to play
So mummy made a box for her
With cards for every day

Every day she will pick one
The card will then say
What she will do now
What game she should play

The card she picks has a chest on
Dressing up is her game today
Mummy is bringing the clothes down
It will be a fun day

Look, Sarah is already wearing something
A helmet, a coat and waterspout
O, Sarah is a fireman
She is looking very proud!

An eye patch and a bandana
And a big sharp sword
She looks like a pirate from a book,
Arrr matey, step on board!

Look, she already took it off
and chose a different dress
With a beautiful hat and rosy cheeks
She is a lovely looking princess!

When the clothes are tidied away
And nothing is left on the floor
Then Sarah is Sarah again
Exactly how she was before

The clock says six
And it is the end of the day
Daddy comes home from work
Then she knows, it's dinnertime after play

When she has finished her dinner
And the dishes have been done
Sarah will have bath time
And has to put her pyjamas on

Sarah will now go to sleep
Dreaming of the lovely day
She dreams of dressing up again
And other things she will play

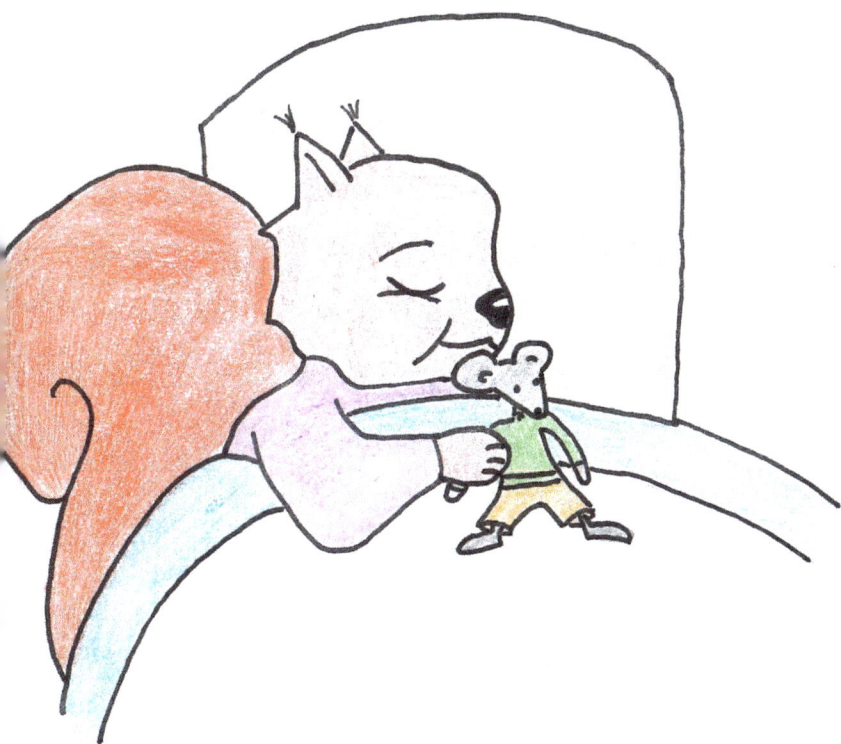

About this book

Children with autism are often taught they have to adjust to our world and perceptions, because they play, communicate and take things in differently. As a mum, I have been experiencing that 'different' isn't always easy, but can be beautiful if you keep an open mind to it. Like the poet Hans Andreus beautifully expresses in his poem:

"You are so beautifully different than I am, no more or less, but just beautifully different, I would never want you any differently different."

I was looking for a book that took into account the language- and stimulus processing of children with autism. A book where children with autism can recognise themselves in the main character of the book. Where they'll say; "That's how it happens at my house too, or, that's how I play too." A book with illustrations in adapted colours, where the characters do not look the reader straight in the eye and written from their perception. That's how the story about Sarah arose.

I wish all parents and children with or without autism a lot of fun reading the story about Sarah.

Finally, I would like to thank my son Marijn for everything he teaches me about his special world and my husband for confiding in me.

www.ingramcontent.com/pod-product-compliance
Lightning Source LLC
Chambersburg PA
CBHW040805150426
42813CB00056B/2665